Brain Waves
Bible Activities
Age 5-7

Louis Fidge

Contents

3. *Introduction and teachers' notes*

Learning about the Bible
5. The Bible is like a letter
6. The Bible is like a library
7. The Bible is like a lamp

Life in Jesus' time
8. Homes
9. Work
10. Clothes
12. Some Bible animals

Rules
13. God's rules

Poetry and wisdom
14. Psalm 23
15. Proverbs
16. Bible alphabet

Noah
20. Noah and the animals
21. Promises

Joseph
22. Jacob's family
23. Joseph's coat
24. Joseph's dream
25. Joseph's brothers

Moses
26. The baby in the bulrushes
27. A special job for Moses

Joshua
28. Joshua - getting ready
29. Joshua - getting set
30. Joshua - getting going

Samuel
31. Hannah's story
32. Samuel in the temple
33. Listening carefully

David
34. Best of friends
35. David and Goliath

Daniel
36. In the lion's den

Jesus
37. My Advent Calendar
39. Growing up
40. At the temple
41. Jesus the carpenter
42. Jesus' special friends
43. Disciple puppets
44. Can you see?
45. The lost sheep
46. The loving father
47. Caring and sharing
48. Jesus and prayer

Folens books are protected by international copyright laws. All rights reserved. The copyright of all materials in this book, except where otherwise stated, remains the property of the publisher and author(s). No part of this publication may be reproduced, stored in a retrieval system, or transmitted, in any form or by any means, for whatever purpose, without the written permission of Folens Limited.

Folens do allow photocopying of selected pages of this publication for educational use, providing that this use is within the confines of the purchasing institution.

This resource may be used in a variety of ways; however, it is not intended that teachers or students should write directly into the book itself.

© 1994 Folens Limited, on behalf of the author.

First published 1994 by Folens Limited, Albert House, Apex Business Centre, Boscombe Road, Dunstable, LU5 4RL, England.

ISBN 1 85276597-6

Editor: Angela Simms.
Cover: Hybert Type and Design.
Cover photo: Royal Commission for Historical Monuments.
Printed by Craft Print Pte Ltd, Singapore

Teachers' notes

As the Bible is the cornerstone of Christianity it is important that children learn about it in an educationally sound way. Many teachers feel diffident about teaching RE because of:
- their own lack of knowledge
- their personal commitment to a set of religious beliefs
- the lack of flexible, accessible classroom resources.

Brain Waves *Bible Activities* help to resolve these dilemmas. Whilst the activities are clearly based on the Bible, they are primarily educational resources. The material is presented in a non-proselytising way and no particular religious commitment is required or expected of the teacher. Activities focus on:
- the content of the Bible (the characters, stories and and events)
- the context of the Bible (the social, historical and geographical setting)
- knowledge about the book itself (its origins, style composition and themes).

The activities may be used solely for RE lessons, with potential for follow-up work. Alternatively, they may be the starting point for extended topics involving cross-curricular work.
The book includes a wide variety of stimulating:
- writing and discussion activities
- ideas for making simple masks, models, finger puppets
- quizzes and games.

Children are challenged to think about the underlying principles and meanings of stories and events. Wherever possible, children are encouraged to relate the activities to their own lives.

Many of the activities are based specifically on passages and stories from the Bible. The Good News version of the Bible has been used for simplicity. Where appropriate, Bible references are provided so that the activity may be contextualised. The teacher could read the relevant passage for background information. They may choose to re-tell the material in their own words, or adapt the passage to suit the children's needs. With younger children, the former approach is particularly effective.

Notes for individual sheets
Learning about the Bible (pages 5-7).
These activities explain a little about the nature of the Bible. Children learn that Christians believe it is God's word and a code to live by. They also discover that the Bible is a combination of sixty-six books.

Life in Jesus' time (pages 8-12).
This section contextualises the Bible by focusing on some aspects of everyday life. The sheets on *Homes*, *Work*, *Clothes*, and *Some Bible animals* all ask the children to compare and question their own experiences with those of a different culture and historical period. These sheets may also help develop a concept of the past and complement work being done in History.

Rules (page 13).
This sheet deals with the Ten Commandments. Introduce this subject by talking about things we are, and are not allowed to do at home or at school, and why these rules are necessary. An example of a set of rules is those on Road Safety. These are easily explained to children.

Poetry and Wisdom (pages 14-19).
The *Psalms* and *The Book of Proverbs* provide some examples of poetry. Even at a young age children can appreciate, understand and talk about the beauty of the 23rd Psalm. It may be possible to compare the modern version with that in the King James' Bible.

The sheet of proverbs includes a few simple sayings. Children may be able to share some other well-known proverbs or sayings with the rest of the class.

A Bible Alphabet (pages 16-19).
This alphabet covers many characters and topics from the Bible. The sheets may be used in a variety of ways. They may be looked at and discussed as a whole. Return to different aspects of the topics as they arise throughout the year. Another idea is to take each sheet separately and deal with them over the course of four RE lessons. Letters may be considered one at a time, the illustrations coloured and discussed in more depth. They could be used to accompany and reinforce phonic work in English classes.

Teachers' notes

Noah (pages 20-21).
Children may be familiar with some aspects of the story of Noah. Explain that the Bible tells us the flood was sent because the majority of people were mistreating each other and the environment. If appropriate, discuss current global environmental concerns such as pollution. Bring out the concept of the trust that Noah had in God.

Joseph (pages 22-25).
These activities provide an ideal vehicle for considering family relationships and tensions. There was obviously much arguing and bad feeling in Joseph's family, and these sheets cover the issues of jealousy, favouritism, hatred and anger. One sheet also looks at dreams. Later events demonstrate, according to biblical perspectives, that Joseph's enslavement was all part of God's long term plan for the immediate family and for the Jewish nation as a whole.

Moses (pages 26-27).
It would be helpful to do some preliminary work on the story of Moses, introducing the idea that the Israelites had gone to Egypt to escape from famine in their own country, but became slaves who were badly treated. The Pharaoh felt threatened by the growth of the Israelite population and had issued an edict to execute all baby boys. Ask the children to imagine Moses' parents terrible anguish and their uncertainty about leaving him. The concepts of faith and trust are brought out in the second sheet.

Joshua (pages 28-30).
After their desert wanderings, the Israelites stood on the threshold of the Promised Land, the realisation of God's promise to them. Imagine their excitement and anxiety and the fear of the unknown. They were led by Joshua, a prudent and wise leader. Stress the planning and preparation that went into his campaign. Again the idea of faith and trust in God is rewarded.

Samuel (pages 31-33).
The story of Hannah is ideal for talking about spitefulness, anguish, patience, joy and obedience. Samuel was seen as a gift from God and was dedicated to serve him in the temple. Eli took over the pastoral care of Samuel. Imagine Samuel's loneliness on first entering the temple.

Discuss the function of the temple as God's house. The idea of talking to God and the possibility of God talking to us may be difficult for children to grasp. Explain that many Christians believe this is possible. Bring out the humour of Samuel's mistake and how Eli may have thought Samuel was dreaming.

David and Goliath (pages 34-35).
This classic story addresses the issue of fear and bravery in the face of overwhelming odds. The biblical teaching that David had God on his side is reinforced by later events (David becoming King). David's relationship with Jonathan allows the subject of friendship to be explored.

Daniel (page 36).
Cast in the same heroic mould as David, Daniel, with faith and trust in God faced and survived an encounter with the lions. Intrigue and jealousy are issues which could be discussed.

Jesus (pages 37-48).
Christians believe Jesus is the key figure in the Bible. In this section of the book a number of aspects of Jesus' life are considered.

The Advent (which literally means the 'coming') Calendar is an ideal way for recounting the nativity story. Christ's ministry did not begin until he was about thirty, and we know very little of the intervening years. One story from the Bible, the visit to the Temple, gives some insight into the fact that Jesus was no ordinary child. The Bible tells us that Joseph, Jesus' earthly father, was a carpenter and that Jesus followed this trade until his ministry. Explain that Christians believe Jesus to be the Son of God.

Jesus formed a group of special friends, his disciples, who were very ordinary people in many ways. Apart from Judas, the others learnt from his example and later formed the nucleus of the early church.

The sheet on the healing of blind Bartimaeus and the feeding of the five thousand are both examples of recorded miracles. The Bible explains that these demonstrations of Jesus' power over nature were intended to show people God's power. Children could try to imagine the reactions of the various people who were involved.

Story-telling was an important part of Jesus' teachings. The stories Jesus told were parables, which are often enigmatic and allow for a variety of interpretations. Jesus used everyday situations to illustrate his stories, thus a shepherd appeared in one and a wayward son and his loving father in another. These are symbolic of God and his relationships with us. At this stage it is important for children to gain a literal understanding of the relationships involved.

In **Samuel**, the idea of talking to God was introduced. The final activity explains that prayer is seen as a way of communicating with God.

The Bible is like a letter

- Do you like receiving letters, notes and cards? Why?
- Why do people write to each other?
- Write your name and address on this envelope.

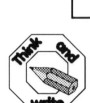

- Work out what this message says.

- Write it out correctly.

```
The Bible is like

        Christians believe

what God wants to say.

it tells them

        a letter from God.
```

_____

_____

_____

_____

_____

Write a letter to a grown up. Tell them what you have learnt about the Bible.

The Bible is like a library

Things to do
- What sort of things would you find in each of these books?
- Match the sentences with the pictures.

| It helps me to find out what words mean. | I can read stories in this book. | It tells me about the the past. |

 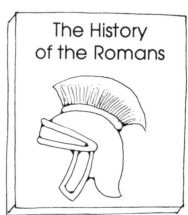 

| It tells me how to to cook. | It tells me where places are. | I can read poems in this book. |

A bible is like a library. It contains sixty-six different books.

Things to do
- Look in a Bible and find the different books. Did you count all sixty-six?

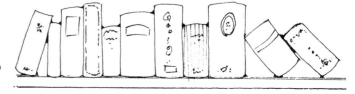

BRAIN WAVES *Bible Activities 5-7.* F5976   © Folens.

The Bible is like a lamp

Psalm 119 verse 105

Christians believe the Bible is like a lamp. It shows them the right way to go.

- Make a list of other sorts of lighting.

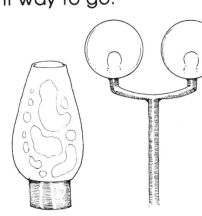

- Cut out the pieces of the jigsaw. Put them together. What have you made?

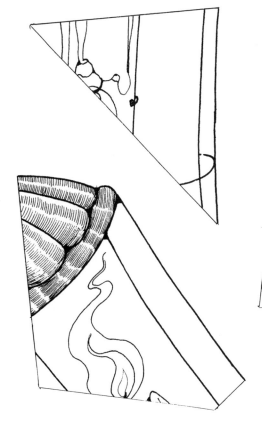
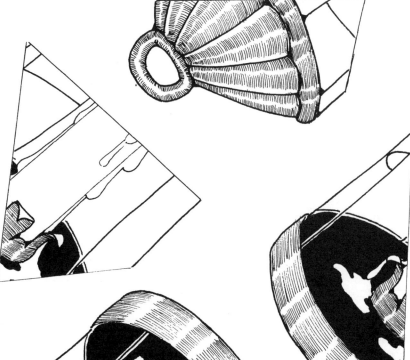

© Folens.   BRAIN WAVES Bible Activities 5–7. F5976

Homes

Now

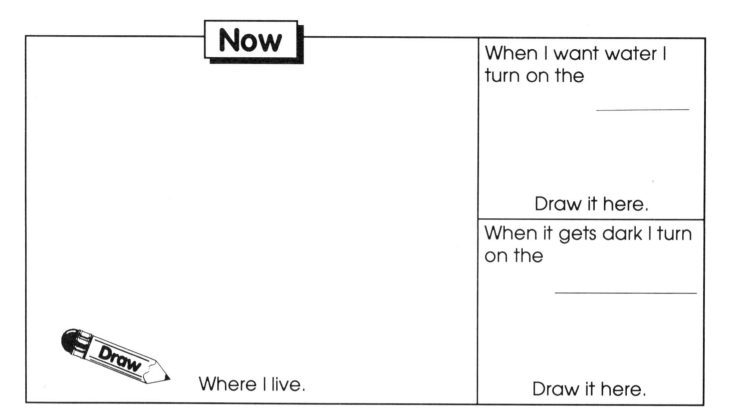

Where I live.

When I want water I turn on the _____

Draw it here.

When it gets dark I turn on the _____

Draw it here.

In Jesus' time

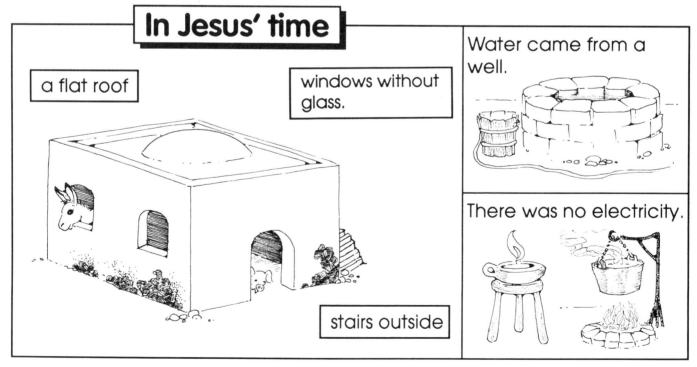

- a flat roof
- windows without glass.
- stairs outside

Water came from a well.

There was no electricity.

- Talk about how houses have changed since Jesus' time.

Work

- Match the labels with the pictures:

fisherman

priest

carpenter

farmer

- What sort of things would these people have done?

Extra — Think of jobs that would not have existed in Jesus' time. Draw and label some pictures of them.

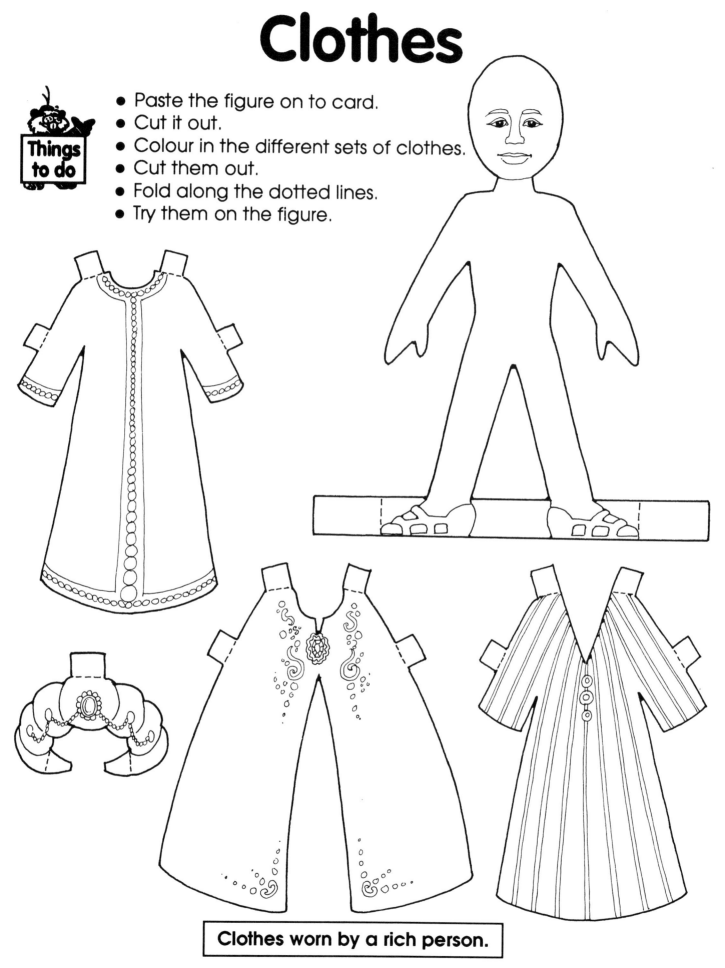

Clothes worn by a poor villager.

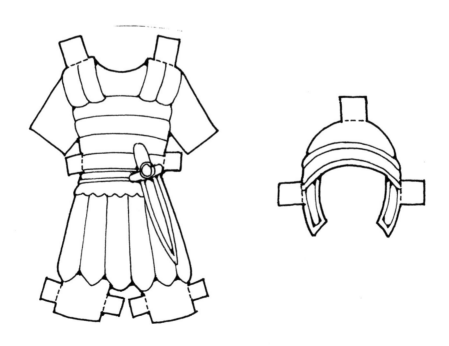

Clothes worn by a Roman soldier.

Some Bible animals

Things to do

- Find the animals' names in the wordsearch.
- Match each name to a picture.
- Write the animal's name under the picture.
  The first one has been done for you.

a	f	d	o	n	k	e	y	m
b	c	a	m	e	l	g	h	j
i	k	o	r	s	h	e	e	p
d	f	g	o	x	e	n	t	s
g	i	g	e	n	k	n	r	t
a	b	e	h	o	r	s	e	n
c	o	a	t	x	g	o	a	t
s	h	c	h	i	c	k	e	n

camel

Can you see all these animals in your own country?
Find some other animals in the Bible.

God's rules

Sharin sees some crisps. She loves crisps. She is tempted to take them. What should she do?

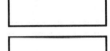
Yes or No

Take them and keep quiet?

Take them and blame someone else?

Leave them alone?

Talk about

- What do you think about stealing and telling lies?

Exodus Chapter 20 verses 1-17

In the Bible there are some simple rules to help people. One of them is to love your parents.

- Find out what the other rules are.

Things to do

- Make a thank you card for a person who looks after you.

TO

Thank you for looking after me.
From

© Folens.   BRAIN WAVES *Bible Activities 5-7.* F5976   13

Psalm 23

This psalm talks about God being like a shepherd.

- Read the poem.
- Talk about what it means.

The Lord is my shepherd;
I have everything I need.
He lets me rest in fields of green grass
And leads me to quiet pools of fresh water.
He gives me new strength.
He guides me to the right paths,
As he has promised.
Even if I go through the deepest darkness,
I will not be afraid Lord,
For you are with me,
Your shepherd's rod and staff protect me.

Proverbs

The Book of Proverbs in the Bible is full of wise sayings.

- Match the sayings to the pictures.

Hot tempers cause arguments. (Proverbs Chapter 15 verse 18)

If you listen to advice, one day you will be wise. (Proverbs Chapter 19 verse 20)

Selfishness only causes trouble. (Proverbs Chapter 28 verse 25)

Smiling faces make you happy. (Proverbs Chapter 15 verse 30)

Pay attention to what you are taught and you will be successful. (Proverbs Chapter 15 verse 30)

You do yourself a favour when you are kind. (Proverbs Chapter 11 verse 17)

© Folens.   BRAIN WAVES *Bible Activities 5-7*. F5976

Bible alphabet (Aa-Ff)

- Colour in the pictures and talk about the Bible stories.

Aa is for the animals in the ark.

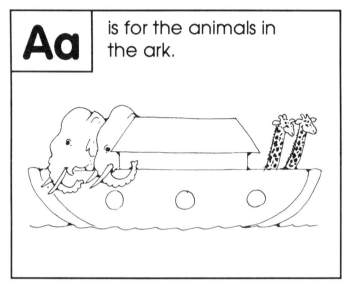

Bb is for baby Moses in a basket in the bulrushes.

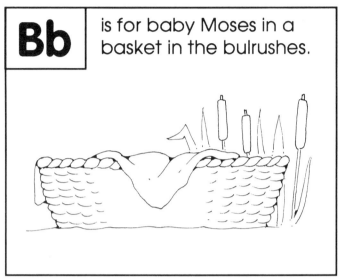

Cc is for Joseph's coat of many colours.

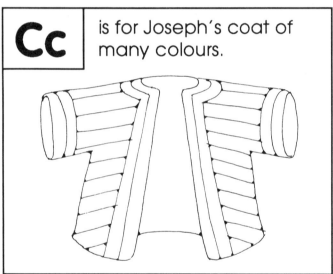

Dd is for Daniel in the lion's den.

Ee is for escape from Egypt.

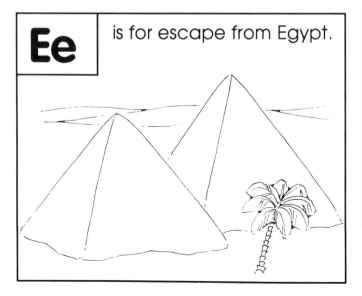

Ff is for fisherman and farmers.

Bible alphabet (Gg-Ll)

Gg is for God.

Hh is for houses and homes in the Holy Land.

Ii is for the infant Jesus at the inn.

Jj is for joy in Jerusalem when Jesus arrived.

Kk is for kindness.

Ll is for lanterns, lamps and lights.

Bible alphabet (Mm-Rr)

Mm is for musical instruments and mountains.

Nn is for Noah.

Oo is for oxen in the fields.

Pp is for priests and prayer.

Qq is for questions.

Rr is for the Romans.

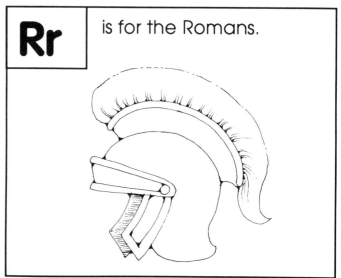

Bible alphabet (Ss–Zz)

Ss is for the shepherd and his sheep.

Tt is for the temple.

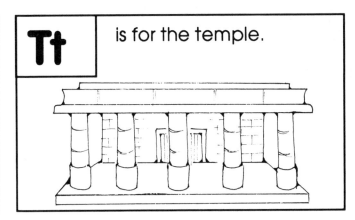

Uu is for the universe.

Vv is for the vineyards in the valley.

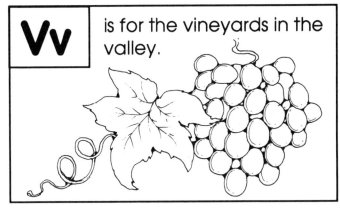

Ww is for water in the well.

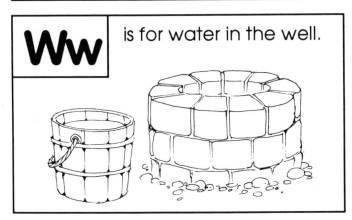

Xx is for King Xerxes.

Yy is for the yoke oxen wear.

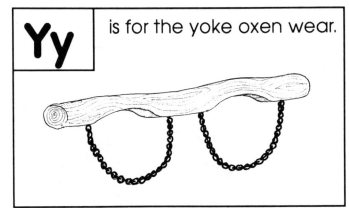

Zz is for Zacchaeus up the tree.

Noah and the animals

Genesis Chapter 6 verses 9-12

- Colour the picture.

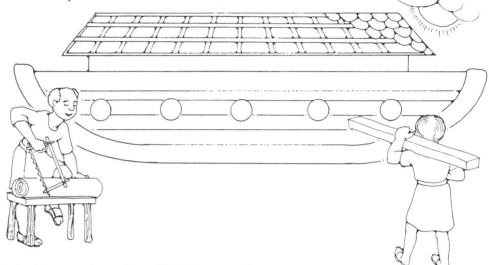

- Match the animals with the outlines.

Promises

Talk about
- Why is it important to keep promises?
- Have you ever broken a promise?

Draw pictures of three people you trust.

Genesis Chapter 9 verses 8-17

Noah trusted God completely. God made Noah a promise.

Things to do
- Can you remember the colours of the rainbow?
- Colour the picture using these colours.

Extra

What did the rainbow mean?
When do rainbows appear? Why?

Jacob's family

Talk about
- How many people are there in your family?
- Do you ever have arguments?

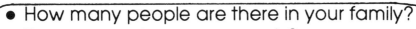

Genesis Chapter 37 verses 1-11

Joseph had eleven brothers and one sister.

- Talk about some of the problems of having a large family.

Things to do
- Arrange the children in Jacob's family in order of size.

Extra! Measure the height of other children in your class. Draw a graph to show their heights, the tallest first.

Joseph's coat

Genesis Chapter 37

 a present you would love to have.

- Why were Joseph's brothers jealous?
- What makes you jealous?

- Join the dots to find Joseph's present.
- Colour it in using bright colours.

Extra Write about what happened to Joseph. Act out his story.

Joseph's dream

 **Talk about**
- Have you ever had a bad dream?
- What did you dream about?

 your dream.

 **Talk about**

Genesis Chapter 37 verses 5-11

- What was Joseph's first dream?
- Why did it make his brothers angry?

 **Things to do**
- Cut out the sun, moon, stars and Joseph.
- Make your own picture.

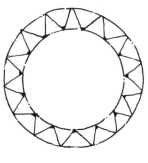

24   BRAIN WAVES *Bible Activities 5-7*. F5976   © Folens.

Joseph's brothers

Talk about
- What makes you really angry?
- What do you think about telling lies?

Genesis Chapter 37 verses 12-35

- Joseph's brothers hated him. What did it make them do?

 how Jacob felt when he heard the news about Joseph.

Things to do
- Colour the picture.
- Make a class camel train to show how Joseph travelled to Egypt.

The baby in the bulrushes

Exodus Chapter 2 verses 1-10

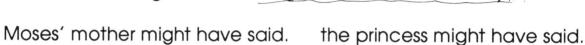

- Write something:

Moses' mother might have said.   the princess might have said.

- Cut out and make Moses' basket.
- Draw a picture of Moses and place it in the basket.
- Write the story and display it with your picture.

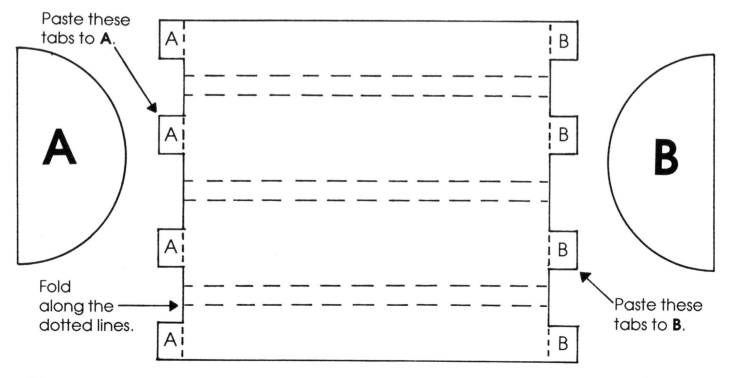

Paste these tabs to **A**.

Fold along the dotted lines.

Paste these tabs to **B**.

A special job for Moses

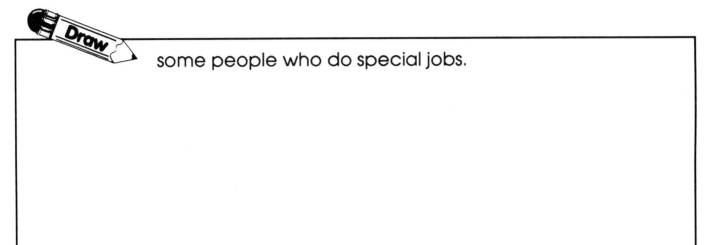

Draw some people who do special jobs.

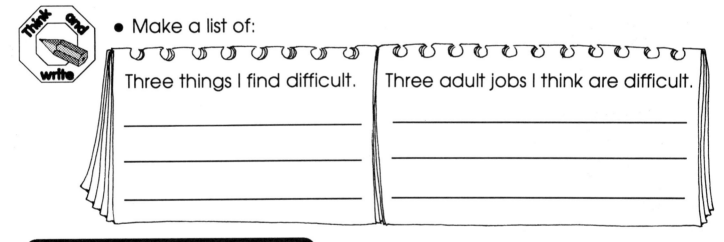

- Make a list of:

Three things I find difficult.

_____
_____
_____

Three adult jobs I think are difficult.

_____
_____
_____

Exodus Chapter 3 verses 1-12

God asked Moses to do something special for him. Moses thought he could not do it. God gave Moses the confidence to do it.

- Think about what fire looks like and colour in the burning bush.

Joshua - getting ready

- How many people are hiding? _____

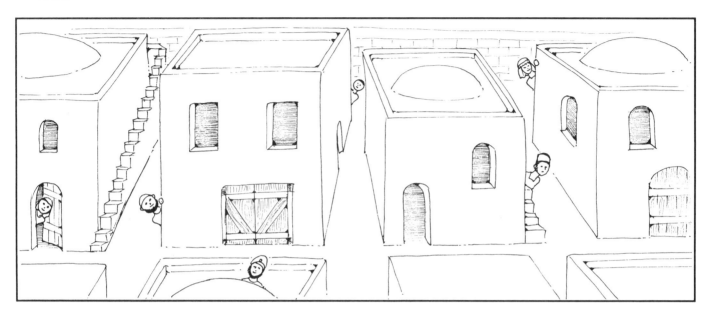

Joshua Chapter 2

- Use the code to work out what Joshua sent the spies to do.

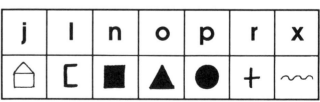

a	c	d	e	g	h	i
△	□	○	☼	⊡	⍋	⊙

j	l	n	o	p	r	x
⌂	[	■	▲	●	+	~

Pretend you are one of the spies.
Write about what you discovered.

Joshua - getting set

When you go on holiday you need to:

 choose where to go    get the tickets.

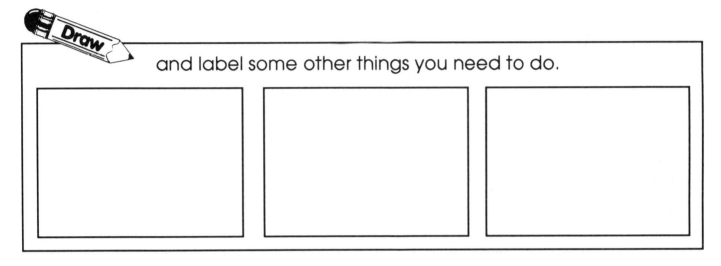

and label some other things you need to do.

Joshua Chapter 3

- Imagine you are an Israelite. Write to a friend. Tell them about the amazing thing that happened at the river.

Dear _____

_____

_____

_____

_____

_____

_____

Continue over the page.

Joshua - getting going

- Name these musical instruments.

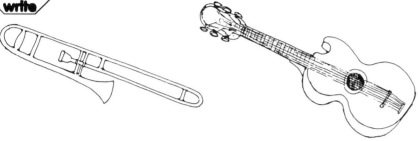

- Explain how each one works.

Joshua Chapter 6 verses 1-20

Something very strange happened when we played our trumpets at Jericho!

- Cut out the bricks.
- Put the sentences in order.

The city had strong stone walls.

The people of Jericho locked themselves inside the city.

The priests blew their trumpets and the soldiers shouted. The walls came tumbling down.

On the seventh day, the Israelites marched around Jericho seven times.

Joshua and the Israelites marched around Jericho every day for six days.

Hannah's story

Things to do
- Think of something kind to say to:
  - a friend
  - someone you do not like
  - someone at home
  - your teacher.

Samuel Book 1 Chapter 1

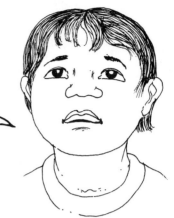

"I get teased because I can not skip."

Draw

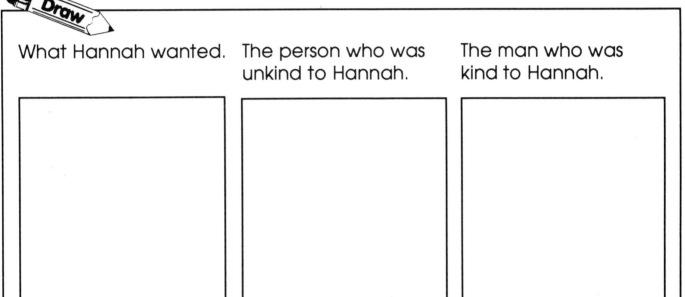

| What Hannah wanted. | The person who was unkind to Hannah. | The man who was kind to Hannah. |

Talk about
- Who did Hannah talk to when she had a problem?
- Who do you talk to when you have a problem?

Extra Join the dots.

'Samuel means 'Name of God'

Make a list of other names and find out what they mean.

Samuel in the temple

- Match the labels to the jobs.

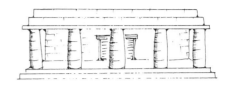

  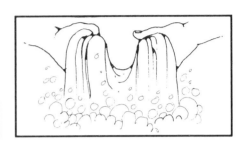

washing   cooking   gardening

- Who does these jobs at home?
- What jobs do you help with?

Samuel Book 1 Chapter 2 verses 18-20

Samuel came to live in the temple and help me.
- Match up the sentences and write them in the correct order.

The temple was	People came here
Candle and lights reminded	The priest and his helpers
to talk and pray together.	made it a warm, friendly place.
a meeting place.	people it was God's house.

Listening carefully

- Listen carefully for a minute. Tick which of these you heard.

Samuel Book 1 Chapter 3 verses 1-10

God spoke to Samuel. God said Samuel would become a great leader.

- Write what Eli said to Samuel every time he misheard God's voice:

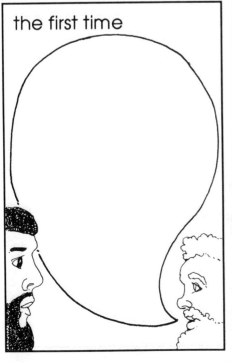

the first time

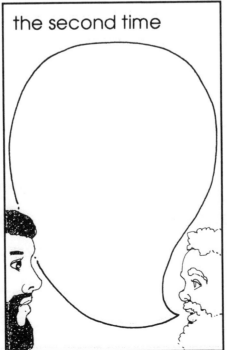

the second time

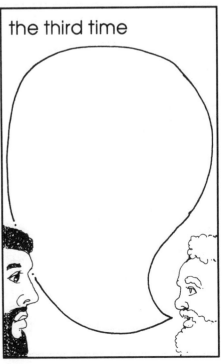

the third time

Best of friends

- Fill in the friendship file.

My name is _____

Draw

me

Some things I like:
_____
_____

My friend's name is _____

Draw

my friend

Some things my friend likes:
_____
_____

Samuel Book 1 Chapter 18 verses 1-5

David and Jonathan were good friends.

- What sort of things do you think they did and said?

- Write a friendship poem.

A Friendship Poem

Friendship means telling each other secrets.

Friendship means sharing our sweets.

Friendship means _____

Friendship _____

David and Goliath

• Join the dots and find out what I am afraid of.

• What frightens you?

Samuel Book 1 Chapter 17

 a picture of a giant.

 David.

 Measure three metres.

This is how tall Goliath was!

In the lion's den

 the Prime Minister.

 **Talk about**
- Who is our Prime Minister?
- Do you think this is an important job?
- What sort of things does a Prime Minister do?

Daniel Chapter 6

I wanted to make Daniel my Prime Minister, but his enemies had other thoughts.

 **Things to do**
- Paste these figures on to card.
- Cut them out.
- Paste a lollipop stick on to the back of each figure.
- Act out Daniel's story.

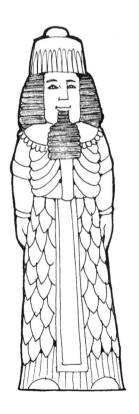

My Advent Calendar

- Cut along the dotted lines and fold the doors back.
- Paste the door sheet carefully on to this sheet so the doors will open.
- Open a door each day and colour the picture.
- Talk about the Christmas story.

Growing up

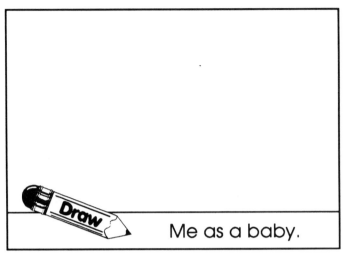
Me as a baby.

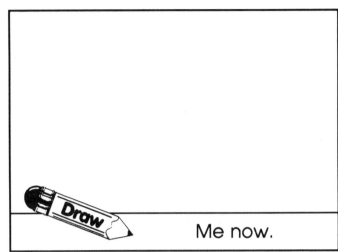
Me now.

Talk about
- How have you changed?
- What things were you able to do when you were a baby?
- What things can you do now?
- What do you want to do when you grow up?

Things to do
- Number the pictures in order.
- Talk about some things that happened to Jesus in his life.

Jesus as a boy.

Jesus teaching about God.

Jesus learning to be a carpenter.

Jesus as a baby.

At the temple

Luke Chapter 2 verses 41-52

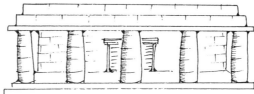

Draw in the missing parts of this picture.

Mary and Joseph discovered Jesus was missing. He was found in the temple.

Draw Jesus talking to some priests.

Talk about
- How do you think Mary and Joseph felt when they found Jesus?
- What was Jesus talking about?
- Why did Jesus call the temple his father's house?

Jesus the carpenter

Things to do
- Colour in the things which Jesus might have made.

Write a list of tools carpenters use today.
Would they have been used in Jesus' time?

Jesus' special friends

Things to do

- How many special friends did Jesus have?
- Did any have the same names? Which were twins?
- Which names are still used today?
- Colour in the pictures. Cut them out. Arrange them in alphabetical order.

 Judas was not a very good friend to Jesus. Find out why.

Disciple puppets

Jesus

Peter

James

John

Andrew

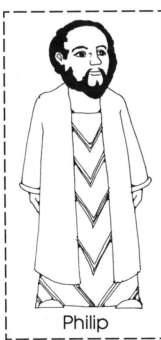
Philip

Bartholomew

Matthew

Things to do

- Colour in the pictures.
- Cut them out.
- Make them into finger or stick puppets.

- Read some Bible stories about Jesus and his friends.
- Make your own puppet theatre and act out the stories.

Can you see?

Things to do
- Spot the differences between these two pictures. Circle them.
- How many are there?
- Compare your answers with a partner.

Mark Chapter 10 verses 46-52

- Think of five things you would miss if you could not see.

Things to do
- Imagine you are blind. Choose one of the jobs in the box. Try to do it with your eyes closed. What problems did you have?

Tying your laces.
Putting on your jumper.
Writing your name.

1. _____
2. _____
3. _____
4. _____
5. _____

BRAIN WAVES *Bible Activities 5-7.* F5976 © Folens.

The lost sheep

Luke Chapter 15 verses 4-9

Talk about
- The work of a shepherd.

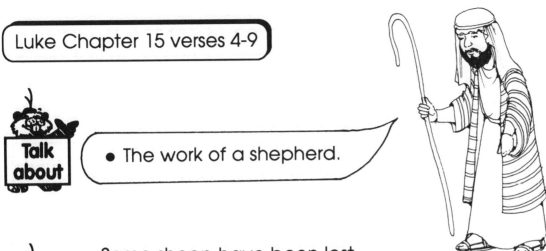

Things to do

Some sheep have been lost.
- Draw along the shepherd's path with a coloured pencil.
- As you find the sheep, colour them in.
- Count how many sheep were lost. Write the number in the sheep pen.

The loving father

Luke Chapter 15 verses 11-32

 the missing pictures and write a sentence to finish the story.

| 1 | The son took the money and left. | 2 | He spent all the money. |

| 3 | After the money had gone, his friends left. | 4 | He had to eat pig's food. |

| 5 | |

Talk about

- Use your pictures to tell the story to a partner.
- Why is it important to say 'I'm sorry'?
- Why is it important to learn to forgive?
- Why do you think Jesus told this story?

Caring and sharing

 some things you would take for a picnic.

• Give each person a cake.

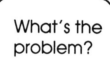 What's the problem?

John Chapter 6 verses 1-15

• What does the story of the boy who shared his food tell you about:
 - the boy?
 - Jesus?

 • Imagine you were the boy. Tell your story to a friend.

Extra Find a way to cut the birthday cake into four equal parts.

Jesus and prayer

- Who have you talked to today? Complete this list.

	✓ or ✗	Draw them	Write their names
Family			
Friends			
Teacher			

Matthew Chapter 6 verses 7-15

Talking to God is called praying. Jesus often talked to God.

- The Bible says we can talk to God about anything.

Things to do

- Write a short prayer thanking God for something.

My 'thank you' prayer